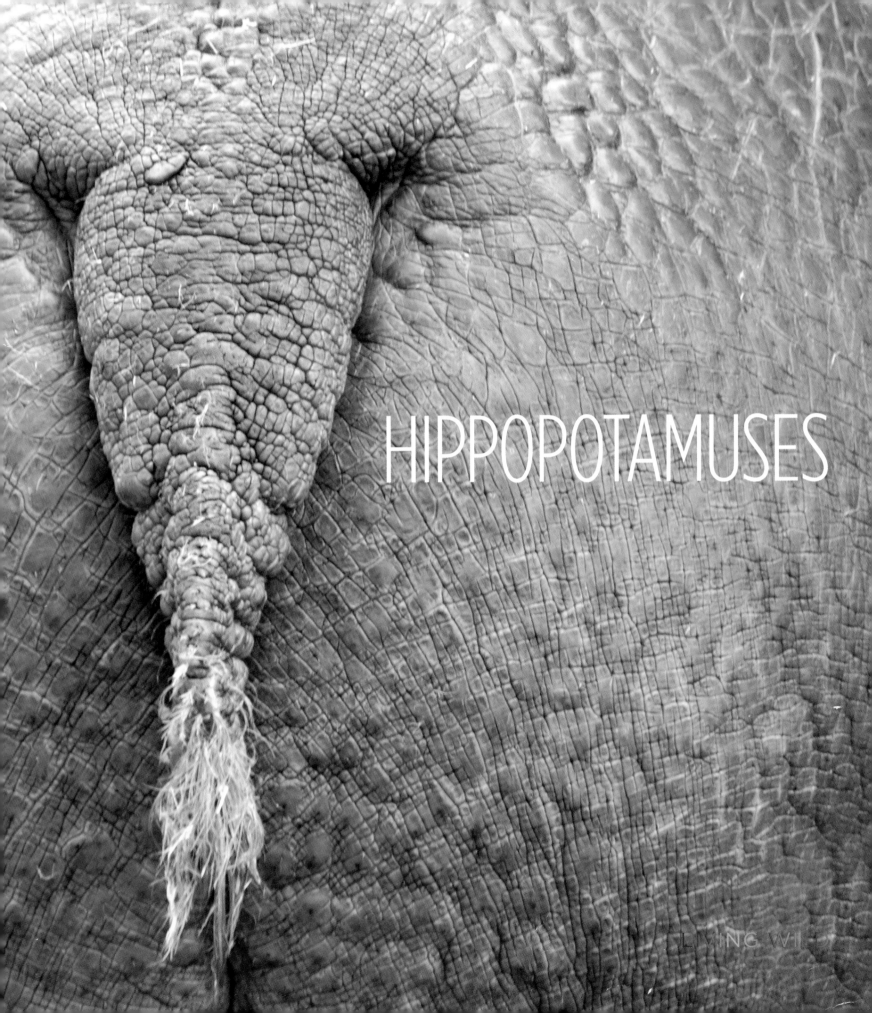

HIPPOPOTAMUSES

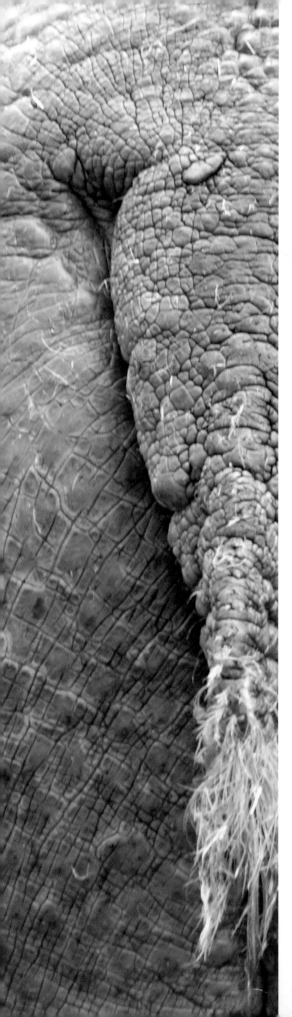

LIVING WILD

Published by Creative Education
P.O. Box 227, Mankato, Minnesota 56002
Creative Education is an imprint of The Creative Company
www.thecreativecompany.us

Design and production by Mary Herrmann
Art direction by Rita Marshall
Printed in the United States of America

Photographs by Alamy (The Art Gallery Collection, Aurora Photos, Michele Burgess, Corbis Super RF, Kypros), Corbis (Bureau L.A. Collection), Disney Wiki (DTierney30), Dreamstime (Crazy80frog, Sam D'cruz, Ferdinandreus, Aleksandr Frolov, Gator, Lizafoto567, Pleprakaymas, Teddykebab, Jiri Vaclavek, Karin Van Ijzendoorn, VGM), Getty Images (RAUL ARBOLEDA/AFP, DEA/G. DAGLI ORTI, Gerald Hinde, Nigel Pavitt), Shutterstock (Chris Alleaume, Civdis, Sam DCruz, Chris Erasmus, hallam creations, magnola, Nazzu, Stu Porter, Nikos Psychogios, J Reineke, Uryadnikov Sergey, Steffen Foerster Photography, thoron, Gary Unwin, warmer, Jan Zoetekouw), Wikipedia (Dave Fischer/Flickr, Julien Willem)

Library of Congress Cataloging-in-Publication Data
Gish, Melissa.
Hippopotamuses / by Melissa Gish.
p. cm. — (Living wild)
Includes index.
Summary: A look at hippopotamuses, including their habitats, physical characteristics such as their large mouths, behaviors, relationships with humans, and protected status in the world today.
ISBN 978-1-60818-288-6
1. Hippopotamidae—Juvenile literature. I. Title.

QL737.U57G57 2013
599.63'5—dc23   2012023244

First Edition
9 8 7 6 5 4 3 2 1

CREATIVE EDUCATION

HIPPOPOTAMUSES

Melissa Gish

Spring rains have swollen the Mara River in Kenya, luring animals to drink and prompting crocodiles to hunt.

Resident hippopotamuses submerged near the riverbank watch their neighbors with curiosity.

S pring rains have swollen the Mara River in Kenya, luring grassland animals to drink and prompting crocodiles to hunt. Resident hippopotamuses submerged near the riverbank watch their neighbors' activities with curiosity. While the gazelles, wildebeest, and even lions appear ever vigilant around the crocodiles, the hippos are fearless when it comes to the massive reptiles. Suddenly, a crocodile leaps from the water and pulls a young gazelle off its feet and into the water. Other crocodiles join in the feeding frenzy. Two hippos, an adult and a baby, wade into the mass of crocodiles. They nudge the reptiles with their noses and nibble on their spiked backs. The young hippo even bites the tail of one of the larger crocodiles. But the crocodiles pay no attention to the hippos. According to the unique relationship that hippos and crocodiles share, the reptiles continue their feast while allowing the hippos to torment them.

WHERE IN THE WORLD THEY LIVE

■ **Common or Nile Hippo**
30 African countries, including Mozambique, Tanzania, Zambia

■ **Pygmy Hippo**
Nigeria, Ivory Coast, Ghana, Sierra Leone

The two hippopotamus species are native to the African continent. Common hippos can still be found in nearly 30 African countries, with concentrations in Mozambique, Tanzania, and Zambia. Pygmy hippos are today found in only four countries. The colored squares on the map below indicate common locations for each species.

RIVER HORSES

As creatures that live in the sea, dugongs possess paddle-like forelimbs and fluked tails similar to dolphins'.

T he common hippopotamus, also called the river or Nile hippopotamus, and its cousin, the pygmy hippopotamus, are members of the order Artiodactyla—hoofed animals with an even number of toes. Among the more than 200 other artiodactyls are pigs, antelopes, cattle, giraffes, and camels. Despite sharing some physical characteristics with these animals, hippopotamuses are more closely related to whales. Scientists believe that a common ancestor of whales and hippopotamuses existed more than 60 million years ago. Then, about 55 million years ago, early whales and hippopotamuses began to **evolve** separately.

Four species of Malagasy hippopotamus once existed on the island of Madagascar, but they are now all **extinct**— the last species disappeared as recently as 1,000 years ago. Populations of common hippopotamus once covered half of Africa, from the Cape of Good Hope all the way north to the Nile River, but now the species' range is limited. It has been driven to extinction in many places, including Egypt, where it was once one of the most abundant species. Today, fewer than 150,000 common hippos and

Hippos are in the company of whales, manatees, and dugongs when it comes to mating underwater.

Since pygmy hippos breed well in captivity, most of the nearly 200 zoo hippos worldwide have been born of captive parents.

no more than 3,000 pygmy hippos are left in the wild. Common hippos can be found in lakes and rivers in nearly 30 countries in Africa, though their numbers are declining in more than a dozen of those nations. The largest hippo populations are located in Mozambique, Tanzania, and Zambia. Scattered populations of pygmy hippos exist in the forests of Nigeria, Côte d'Ivoire (Ivory Coast), Ghana, and Sierra Leone.

The **semiaquatic** hippopotamus, whose name in Greek means "river horse," has a massive barrel-shaped body, four thick legs, and a large head with a mouth capable of opening to a 150-degree angle. A four-foot-tall (1.2 m) person could stand up inside a hippo's open mouth. Despite rivaling the white rhinoceros as the second-heaviest land animal (after the elephant), the common hippopotamus stands only about five feet (1.5 m) tall. Male hippos can be up to 14 feet (4.3 m) long and weigh up to 8,000 pounds (3,629 kg). Females are smaller, averaging lengths of 9.5 feet (2.9 m) and weights of up to 5,000 pounds (2,268 kg). A hippo's tail adds up to 20 inches (50.8 cm) to the animal's length. The much smaller pygmy hippopotamus rarely exceeds 600 pounds (272 kg).

Bull

Despite their massive size, hippos can climb rocky, steep banks, if they can gain sure footing.

Mother hippos are fiercely protective of their calves, especially when they leave the safety of the water to feed.

Adult male hippopotamuses are called bulls, and females are called cows. Baby hippos are called calves.

Hippopotamuses are mammals. All mammals produce milk to feed their young and, with the exceptions of the egg-laying platypuses and hedgehog-like echidnas of Australia, give birth to live offspring. Mammals are also warm-blooded. This means that their bodies try to maintain a healthy, constant temperature. All mammals have hair, but some have more hair than others. Hippos have only sparse, fine hair on their bodies, leaving their tender skin exposed. Hippos live in hot climates and avoid overheating by soaking in water as much as possible— often for as long as 16 hours during the heat of the day.

The nostrils, ears, and eyes are positioned on top of the hippo's head to enable it to breathe and remain alert while most of its body is underwater. When a hippo submerges completely, muscles pinch the nostrils and ears shut to keep water out, and a nictitating (*NIK-tih-tate-ing*) **membrane**, or see-through inner eyelid, protects the hippo's eyes. Young hippos can stay underwater for less than a minute, but an adult hippopotamus can hold its breath for up to five minutes. Four webbed toes on each foot provide stability

Some scientists believe hippos may snort out digestive gases through their nostrils—like burping through their noses.

Webcams allow virtual visitors to see the common hippos at the Toledo Zoo's 360,000-gallon (1.36 million l) Hippoquarium.

A hippo's ivory canine tusks can be as sharp as knives and just as deadly in a fight with another hippo.

Carp use the barbels around their mouths to scrape algae from hippo hides and nibble food from hippo teeth.

when walking over slippery rocks and climbing steep banks. Despite its relatively short legs, a hippopotamus can run on land at speeds of up to 20 miles (32.2 km) per hour.

When the sun goes down and the temperature drops, hippos leave the water to browse for food on land. Hippos are herbivores, meaning they eat plants and grasses, but they also eat soft fruit that falls from trees. They establish trails from their water sources to their feeding grounds. In a single night, a hippo may travel up to six miles (9.7 km) on these trails to find food. Because hippos are inactive except when feeding, they eat no more than 80 to 100 pounds (36.3–45.4 kg) of vegetation per night—only about 1 percent of their body weight. By comparison, the average American eats more than 2 percent of his or her body weight daily. Hippos spend five to six hours feeding at night.

One of the hippo's most striking characteristics is the pair of long canine teeth that protrudes from the lower jaw. Kept sharpened by grinding against the upper teeth, the lower canines continue to grow throughout the hippo's lifetime and can reach up to 20 inches (50.8 cm) in length. The hippo uses these teeth for fighting and defense, not eating. Its strong, hardened lips shear off vegetation, and

Hippos on land will rush immediately to the safety of the closest body of water if they feel threatened.

When watering holes dry up and become muddy pits, hippos defend the areas as they await the return of rain.

wide, flat teeth called molars—located along the sides of the hippo's jaws—grind up the food. Though normally aggressive, hippos are calm when it comes to their teeth and allow birds to sit inside their open mouths to clean out bits of food and **parasites**. In 2010, in what researchers call a "remarkable event," a hippo that was housed with a zebra at Switzerland's Zoo Zurich allowed the zebra to clean its teeth as visitors snapped pictures for 15 minutes.

To keep their skin healthy both in and out of the water, hippos secrete an oily substance from glands located just beneath the surface of their skin. Because this substance is made up of two acids that are red and orange, early observers of hippos believed that the animals were sweating blood. But hippos do not have sweat glands. Rather, holes in the hippo's hide, which are large enough to be seen by the naked eye, release the substance. The secretions protect the hippo's flesh from sunburn and act as an **antibacterial** agent, guarding the hippo against infections that might be caused by bacteria and parasites in its watery habitat. Scientists are now studying the antibacterial properties of hippopotamus secretions for possible use in human medicines.

In addition to their daily diet of grain pellets, fruit, and vegetables, zoo hippos eat about 35 pounds (15.9 kg) of hay.

In 2008, Dr. Brady Barr measured a female hippo's bite force as being 1,821 pounds per square inch (1.28 million kg/sq m).

SINK OR SWIM

P ygmy hippopotamuses generally live alone or in pairs. Common hippopotamuses live in groups but are not considered social animals. With the exception of mothers and calves, common hippos do not form bonds with each other. They live along rivers and lakes in groups called pods that typically consist of up to 30 individuals, including males and females of all ages. A dominant male leads the pod and defends a portion of the river or lake as his territory, marking its boundaries with his **feces** and urine. Other males generally stay out of the dominant male's way. Most leading hippos remain in power for about eight years. Younger, stronger males then challenge the leadership by starting a fight with the dominant male. The opponents open their mouths, exposing their long teeth, and crash their lower jaws together. Hippos have broken their teeth off in this way. Fighting males also bite each other, often causing deep wounds that leave scars.

A hippopotamus's territory consists of a strip of lake or river water and the adjacent bank. Because the water in lakes typically dries up seasonally, hippos protect a

A pod's dominant male vocalizes to ward off rival males who may be too close to his territory.

During dry times of the year, hippos may form pods of up to 200 members to travel great distances in search of water.

Hippos keeping cool in water do not mind having birds such as cormorants rest on their backs to soak up the sun.

large portion of a lake, often about 1,200 feet (366 m) in length. River territories, which have a fairly constant supply of water, are smaller, averaging about 250 feet (76.2 m) in length. On land, grazing areas are considered open to any hippo, so dominant males do not defend any land-based territory. Also, males do not control females, who are free to travel throughout their habitats, often leaving one pod to join another for a time.

Pygmy hippos can reproduce by age 3, their **gestation** period is 6 to 7 months, and newborns weigh about 12 pounds (5.4 kg). Common hippos mature later. Females are old enough to mate when they reach about six or seven

years old. Males are able to mate by age 7, but they usually do not become dominant in a territory until they are at least 10 or 12 years old. Only the dominant male mates with the females currently living in his territory, though he may occasionally allow a limited number of other males access to the females. Adult females typically reproduce every two years. There is no specific mating season for hippos, but mating is closely tied to climate. Hippos that mate in the hot summer months give birth in the spring when the rainy season begins. This ensures that the mothers will have plenty to eat while caring for their calves.

After carrying her young for eight months, a common

Adult hippos cannot swim, but unlike smaller calves, they can use their feet to push off from the river- or lakebed.

hippo cow moves away from the others to give birth. A single calf (twins are rare) may be born on land or underwater. If the mother gives birth on land, she will immediately take her calf into the water. Common hippo newborns are 4 feet (1.2 m) long on average and weigh between 70 and 110 pounds (31.8–50 kg), depending on whether they are female or male, with males being larger. A newborn is mentally bright, alert, and ready for life in the water. Unable to swim, it instinctively allows its mother to push it to the surface to breathe, which it must do every 30 to 40 seconds. For a period of one to two weeks, the mother hippo remains distant from her pod, vocalizing with her offspring to form a bond with it. She will not leave the safety of the water for several days, going without food until her calf is strong enough to walk on land with her.

While calves are more **buoyant** than adults, they cannot float indefinitely. When a mother needs to submerge in water that is too deep for her calf, the young hippo may ride on her back. Until a hippo is large enough to surface on its own, it relies on its mother for help. A calf typically feeds on its mother's milk for up to eight months, but if food is scarce, the calf may not be fully **weaned** for several more months. Calves nurse both on land and underwater. For the first year of its life, a young hippo is totally dependent on its mother for emotional and physical security. A calf learns how to get along in its pod by playing with other calves. By the time it reaches its first birthday, a young hippo will weigh about 500 pounds (227 kg). Female hippos typically remain in the same pod as their mother, while males may eventually leave their families to establish their own territories.

A hippo can roar more loudly than a lion; its roar has been measured at 115 decibels— 1 decibel higher than a lion's.

Like whales that expel water from their blowholes, hippos snort out excess water through their nostrils.

Unlike their larger common hippo cousins, pygmy hippos can make sounds but typically choose to remain silent.

Because hippopotamuses move from group to group, they constantly communicate with each other to indicate their presence. They are the only animals known to make simultaneous sounds underwater (using vibrating layers of fat in the throat) and in the air (using their nostrils). Like their distant relatives the whales, hippos make squeaks, deep grunts, creaking groans, and thunderous rumbles—and a chorus of sounds can travel great distances. Dominant male hippos are especially vocal. While traveling in Africa in 1989, American biologist William Barklow observed that when a dominant male hippo vocalized, males in territories as far as one mile (1.6 m) away responded with their own vocalizations, leading to a chain of communication up and down their river habitat. Barklow speculated that the hippos were communicating their locations—letting other hippos know where territorial boundaries were drawn and helping them avoid making intrusions. Hippos also communicate using infrasound. The **frequencies** of these sound waves are so low that humans can't hear them without the aid of special equipment.

Hippos can live 50 years in the wild and longer in captivity. Adult hippopotamuses have no natural

predators. However, small calves may be singled out for attack by lions or packs of spotted hyenas. When danger approaches, all the hippos in a pod may crowd close to the calves to offer protection. And if a calf is attacked, the other hippos may pursue the aggressor in an attempt to rescue the calf. Crocodiles and hippos have a unique predator-prey relationship. Crocodiles may soak in the water or sun themselves on banks with hippos right next to them and not show any aggression; in fact, observers have spotted crocodiles lying motionless as young hippos licked and nibbled on their tails. Only when calves wander off alone, away from the protection of adults, will crocodiles attempt an attack.

A hippo's underwater vocalizations may sound like whale songs, croaking, or clicking and may not be audible above the surface.

Ancient Egyptian kings made great spectacles of hippopotamus hunts and were even buried with hippo sculptures.

JAWS OF DEATH

Around 100 B.C., ancient Romans, fascinated with Egypt's Nile River and its hippos, depicted them in art.

For thousands of years, humans have interacted with hippos. Anthropologists (scientists who study the history of humankind) discovered evidence at the Bouri Formation, a rich fossil bed in eastern Ethiopia, that human ancestors had hunted and fed on hippos at least 160,000 years ago. In the Sahara Desert of southern Algeria, the Tassili n'Ajjer Mountains contain a vast collection of more than 15,000 cave and rock paintings that were created by humans from about 12,000 until 2,000 years ago. A number of images are of hippopotamuses—and of humans hunting them.

In ancient Egypt, the hippopotamus was a symbol of fertility, and the river goddess Taweret protected mother and child during pregnancy and childbirth. Taweret was depicted as a pregnant hippopotamus that walked on two legs and had the limbs of a lion and the tail of a crocodile. All three animals had reputations for being fiercely protective of their offspring. Small statues and jewelry featuring Taweret were kept in homes to watch over mothers and children. Large statues of Taweret were placed in the burial chambers and pyramids of dead kings to assist

At a site in Namibia, thousands of images of hippos and other creatures were carved into rock as many as 6,000 years ago.

Semiaquatic common hippos do not eat water plants, while land-dwelling pygmy hippos do eat water plants.

the rulers in their rebirth in the afterlife. According to Egyptian **mythology**, Taweret blessed the annual flooding of the Nile River, which provided water to crops.

A folk tale from Nigeria explains why the common hippopotamus lives in the water. Long ago, the hippo was a king, but only his wives knew his name. He hosted many feasts, but he always ended up sending away his guests because they could not call him by name. At one feast, disappointed in his neighbors, the king proclaimed that if any of them could say his name, he would take his wives to live in the water and let his neighbors enjoy the feast for themselves. So the cunning tortoise hid himself while the hippos went to bathe in the river, and he overheard one of the hippo king's wives say the name of her husband. At the next feast, the tortoise said the name of the hippo king: Isantim. True to his word, the hippo king took his wives to the river, and to this day that is where hippos remain.

Pygmy hippopotamuses are the subjects of folklore as well. A story from Liberia tells how the forest-dwelling pygmy hippo carries a brilliant diamond in its mouth to light its path through the forest at night. During the day, the hippo hides the diamond, and if a hunter is lucky

Trees are planted in pygmy hippo enclosures so the animals can scratch their backs, as they do in the wild.

Hyacinth Hippo also appeared in Who Framed Roger Rabbit? (1988) and Mickey's Twice Upon a Christmas (2004).

As of 2013, the oldest hippo in recorded history was Donna (age 61), resident of the Mesker Park Zoo in Evansville, Indiana.

enough to find a pygmy hippo, he may persuade the animal to reveal the diamond's hiding place. While pygmy hippos are shy creatures, common hippos are quite different. The common hippopotamus is one of the most aggressive animals in Africa. In modern times, hippos have attacked and killed more humans in Africa each year than any other wild animal—including crocodiles. But unlike reality, in stories and movies, the hippo has earned a reputation as a large, lovable character, the most recognizable of which may be Hyacinth Hippo and her troupe of hippo ballerinas, who were featured in the 1940 Walt Disney classic *Fantasia*.

In 1953, 10-year-old Gayla Peevey recorded the song "I Want a Hippopotamus for Christmas." The tune's popularity led the Oklahoma City Zoo to launch a fundraiser to "buy a hippo for Gayla." A baby hippopotamus was purchased with the funds, and Peevey attended a ceremony to present the hippo, named Matilda, to the zoo. The song can still be heard on American radio stations around the winter holiday season. In 1964, Hanna-Barbera, the American production company responsible for such television shows as *The Flintstones* and *Scooby-Doo*, produced a short-lived animated series called

Eze the hippo and Duke the kangaroo hatch some mischievous plans in Walt Disney's The Wild *(2006).*

The Peter Potamus Show. Peter Potamus, a friendly, purple hippopotamus, was a time-traveling explorer who, along with a companion named So-So the monkey, journeyed from one historical event to another in a time-traveling hot-air balloon. To get out of trouble, Peter relied on his booming voice, using a special Hippo Hurricane Holler. *The Peter Potamus Show* may now be seen in syndication on the Cartoon and Nicktoons networks. Peter also made special appearances in a number of Yogi Bear cartoons.

The Hungry Hungry Hippos tabletop game was introduced by Hasbro in 1978 and is still available today,

Researchers believe Mzee caught Owen's attention because the tortoise was similar in shape and color to an adult hippo.

though the colors and names of the hippos have changed over the years. The object of the game is to press the tail of a toy hippo, which causes it to open its mouth and consume marbles on a game board. The player whose hippo is the "hungriest"—the one that snaps up the most marbles—wins the game. In the same decade that Hungry Hungry Hippos made its debut, American author and illustrator James Edward Marshall began writing about two hippopotamus friends. In a series of seven books, published from 1972 to 1988, George and Martha shared many adventures and, despite some disagreements, emphasized the value of friendship. Adapted for Canadian television in 1999, the show *George and Martha* ran for 26 episodes. In 2011, a new hippopotamus character was launched by ComboApp, a Canadian video game company. *Hippie Hippo* is a game that challenges players to help the bulky, purple Hippie, who often carries a hockey stick, knock other characters off the Arctic ice. The game also became available as an iPhone/iTouch/iPad® application, and Hippie was also made into a Webkinz stuffed animal.

In real life, an amazing friendship developed between Mzee, a 130-year-old Aldabran tortoise and Owen, a hippo calf stranded by a tsunami in Southeast Asia in 2004. After being rescued, Owen was housed with Mzee at Haller Park in Kenya. During their two-year relationship, the hippo and tortoise—who were roughly the same size— ate, slept, and even played together. Once Owen grew too big for Mzee, he was moved to an enclosure with another hippopotamus, but their story was captured in a series of books: *Owen and Mzee: The True Story of a Remarkable Friendship* (2006), *Owen & Mzee: The Language of Friendship* (2007), and *Owen & Mzee: Best Friends* (2007). Visitors to their website, www.owenandmzee.com, can read about the animals and see them in a number of videos.

The Hungry Hungry Hippos are named Sweetie Potamus (pink), Veggie Potamus (green), Bottomless Potamus (yellow), and Picky Potamus (orange).

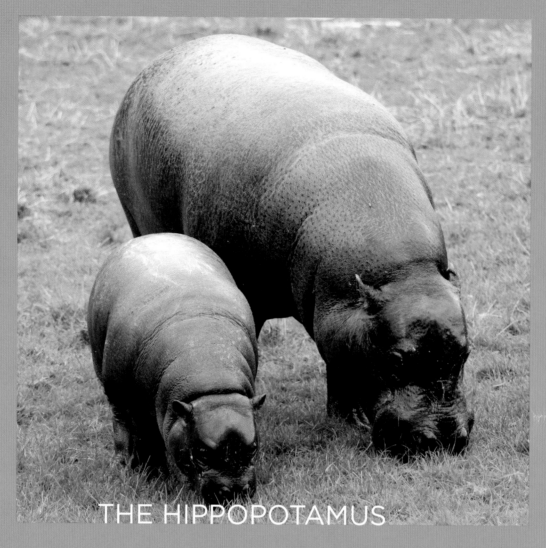

THE HIPPOPOTAMUS

"Oh, say, what is this fearful, wild

 In-cor-ri-gible cuss?"

"This *crea-ture* (don't say 'cuss,' my child;

 'T is slang)—this crea-ture fierce is styled The Hip-po-pot-am-us.

 His curious name de-rives its source

 From two Greek words: *hippos*—a horse,

 Potamos—river. See?

 The river's plain e-nough, of course;

 But why they called that thing a horse,

 That's what is Greek to me."

by Oliver Herford (1863–1935)

A BAD REPUTATION

P ygmy hippos play an important role in their forest **ecosystem**, eating a variety of plants and fruits whose seeds are later dispersed throughout the forest in the hippos' dung. Pygmy hippos are sensitive to changes in their environment, particularly **encroachment** by humans, **deforestation**, and the breaking up of forestland through agricultural development. The pygmy hippopotamus is listed as an endangered species on the Red List of Threatened Species that is published annually by the International Union for Conservation of Nature (IUCN). Most conservation efforts are concentrated in Liberia, where the majority of pygmy hippos exist. In 1983, the government of Liberia recognized the need for the pygmy hippo's protection and designated a 509-square-mile (1,318 sq km) area of the Sapo Forest as Sapo National Park, the country's first national park. The Zoological Society of London's EDGE (Evolutionarily Distinct and Globally Endangered) program is spearheading an effort to count hippos in and around the park using cameras that automatically take pictures when animals pass in front of them. This will aid in the society's study of the

Hippos avoid fast-flowing water, so still lakes or slow-moving rivers are the most ideal hippo habitats.

Pygmy hippos can stand up on their hind legs to reach fruit and leaves, but common hippos are too heavy to hoist themselves up.

Farmers use bright lights to ward off raiding hippos, but sometimes the animals charge rather than run away.

threats facing the hippos, and the information could be used to develop a conservation plan partially funded and enforced by the Liberian government. While pygmy hippos are legally protected from hunting and human disturbance in Sapo National Park, **poaching** still occurs.

Listed on the IUCN Red List as vulnerable, the common hippo's populations are healthy at this time, but continued threats and lack of greater conservation efforts could drive hippo numbers down to dangerously low levels within the next decade. The hippopotamus's greatest threat is humans. Poaching is a serious problem for hippos, whose large teeth have become popular sources of ivory, now that anti-poaching laws that protect elephants are being more strictly enforced. Elephant ivory is highly valuable on the black market, but poaching elephants is risky business, since the animals roam out in the open. Hippos, on the other hand, can be shot from some distance away. Poachers then simply wait for the **carcass** to drift away from the hippo pod to retrieve it. The teeth are sawed off, and the flesh is butchered and sold as **bushmeat**.

Poaching is not the only challenge hippos face. Because hippos thrive in areas of slow-moving fresh water with nearby grassy plains, they must compete with humans for some of the most desirable land in Africa. Hippos are continuously crowded out of their habitats by agriculture and human development. As human populations continue to expand into wilderness areas, hippos are forced into having more contact with people, which often leads to conflict and loss of life on both sides. Researchers believe that up to 300 people die each year from being attacked by hippos, and in most cases, the hippos were taken by surprise and acted defensively, particularly females with

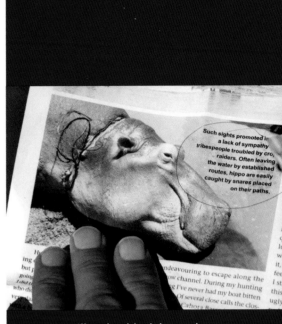

Illegal gold mining and poaching for meat threaten the last remaining pygmy hippos in Sapo National Park.

Hippos have been known to raid farmers' sugar cane and corn crops when other food sources are scarce.

The Republic of Guinea in western Africa issued a stamp featuring the hippo as part of its 1975 Wild Animals series.

South African Voortrekkers, or pioneers, made whips out of strips of hippo hide rubbed with fat, which they used to drive their oxen.

calves. Scientists are working to find ways of keeping hippos and humans safe from one another.

While hippos are highly territorial and protective of their young, healthy hippos rarely launch unprovoked attacks. Biologist and hippo expert William Barklow suggests that the hippo's killer reputation may be exaggerated. If a canoe or small boat approaches hippo territory too closely, hippos may ram the vessel, capsizing it and sending its occupants into the water. Poor swimmers or victims of a fast-moving current may drown, and, despite the fact that the hippos never bit the victims, the hippos are blamed for the related deaths. In 1998, Barklow traveled to Florida to conduct research on hippo communication at Busch Gardens Tampa Bay's Edge of Africa hippo habitat. Using underwater **acoustic** equipment, Barklow continued what has been a decades-long study of the variety, strength, and patterns of hippo vocalizations that are transmitted simultaneously below and above water.

A number of zoos in North America house hippopotamuses and operate **captive-breeding** programs. Hippos tend to breed relatively easily in captivity. The National Zoo in Washington, D.C., has seen more than

20 common hippo and 58 pygmy hippo births since 1931, when the zoo's first captive pygmy hippo was born. More than two-thirds of pygmy hippos born in zoos are females, a situation that could affect conservationists' efforts to maintain genetic diversity in the species through captive-breeding programs. The Institute for Breeding Rare and Endangered African Mammals (IBREAM) and the Royal Zoological Society of Scotland use motion-triggered cameras to capture pictures of pygmy hippo breeding habits in Ivory Coast. By comparing captive behaviors with natural wild behaviors, researchers may learn why captive pygmy hippos give birth to a greater ratio of females to males than do wild pygmy hippos.

As populations of African hippos decline, it is possible that a new group of hippos may thrive across the globe. Centuries ago, as explorers and settlers traveled the world, they took with them many species of plants and animals that eventually flourished in new places. A rare case of hippo transplantation occurred in the small South American country of Colombia, and biologists are studying the animals' effects on the ecosystem there. In 1989, a notorious criminal named Pablo Escobar was arrested and

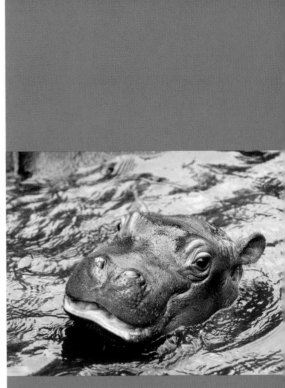

Young hippos without sharp canine teeth have no way of defending themselves and must rely on their mothers for protection.

Elephants and hippos usually get along, but if water becomes scarce, conflict between the species can occur.

sent to prison, forfeiting his 3,700-acre (1,497 ha) ranch to the Colombian government, which then abandoned the ranch. Living on the ranch were three hippos, which Escobar had imported from Africa. While the ranch was deserted for almost 20 years, the hippos lived on their own in the ranch's lagoon and a nearby river, thriving and producing 14 offspring. Then, in 2008, an investment group bought the ranch and turned it into a theme park. The hippos—then numbering 22 individuals—were captured. A study of the hippos and their South American environment continues, as researchers have considered the possibility that some of the original hippos' offspring may remain undetected in the rainforest.

For millions of years, hippopotamuses have been some of the largest members of the African web of life, proving themselves to be vital to the health of their ecosystems. From the tiniest fish that feed on plant matter stuck between hippo teeth to the tallest shrubs grown from seeds dispersed by hippos, many living things depend on hippos. Education and conservation efforts are vital to maintaining strong populations of these magnificent animals for future generations.

A hippo named Orion is one of more than a dozen offspring of hippos once owned by Pablo Escobar.

ANIMAL TALE: THE HUNGRY HIPPO

The Kikuyu people of Kenya have a long tradition of valuing their land and its animals as sources of food, materials, and cultural objects. Many of their folk tales explain why things in nature are so. The following story describes some of the hippopotamus's characteristic behaviors.

Long ago, the creator of all things, N'gai, made the hippopotamus a swift, powerful creature with long, sharp teeth. Living on the open plains and grasslands, the hippo hunted small game and complemented his meals with huge mouthfuls of grass and insects. Finding lots of food and no predators that would attack such a large animal, the hippo grew fatter every day.

"I am big," said the elephant, "but I am not as fat as you."

"You eat too much," said the lion to the hippo. "Save some food for us."

But the hippo did not care that he had been insulted, and he had little regard for his fellow animals.

One day, the elephant and the lion called on N'gai: "Please take the hippo away from here. Make him live in the river or the mountains because he is eating everything, and we are starving."

"I cannot," replied N'gai. "If I move the hippo to the mountains, he will eat all the goats and trees, and if I move him to the river, he will eat all the fish and birds."

The hippo enjoyed his life of plenty, but eventually he found that as he grew fatter he felt hotter. Because he had eaten all the game in the area, he had to travel far under the blazing sun to find antelope to hunt. And because he had eaten all the bushes and trees, there was no shade for him under which to rest.

Every day he trudged to the river for a drink of water, fat and tired, and he watched the fish and birds, wishing he could join them in the river. Finally, the hippo decided to ask N'gai for help. "Please, N'gai," the hippo called out, "the sun is baking me. Let me leave the hot savanna and live in the cool river instead."

"No," N'gai replied. "You have eaten everything within your grasp, leaving nothing for the other animals. If I let you live in the river, you will eat all the fish and birds, too."

So the hippo remained on the sun-baked plains, eating even more to try to satisfy his sadness. But it did not work—the hippo only felt worse. Hot and miserable, he called once again on N'gai. "Please, please," he cried, "save me from this unbearable heat. Put me in the river. I promise that I will not eat all the fish and birds."

"I will allow you to move to the river," said N'gai, "but you must change your eating habits."

"I shall," said the hippo, snapping off his long teeth to prove he would no longer hunt. "And I promise to eat only plants left by other animals."

And from that time on, the hippopotamus remained in the water all day and browsed for plants along the riverbank at night. And to prove that he was not eating any fish or birds, he began to scatter his dung on the shore to show N'gai that no bones could be found in it.

GLOSSARY

acoustic – relating to sound or the sense of hearing

antibacterial – active against bacteria, or living organisms that cannot be seen except under a microscope

buoyant – able to float in water

bushmeat – the meat of wild animals killed for food or for sale in tropical parts of the world such as Asia and Africa

captive-breeding – being bred and raised in a place from which escape is not possible

carcass – the dead body of an animal

deforestation – the clearing away of trees from a forest

ecosystem – a community of organisms that live together in an environment

encroachment – movement into an area already occupied

evolve – to gradually develop into a new form

extinct – having no living members

feces – waste matter eliminated from the body

frequencies – the measurements of sound waves

gestation – the period of time it takes a baby to develop inside its mother's womb

membrane – a thin, clear layer of tissue that covers an internal organ or developing limb

mythology – a collection of myths, or popular, traditional beliefs or stories that explain how something came to be or that are associated with a person or object

parasites – animals or plants that live on or inside another living thing (called a host)

poaching – hunting protected species of wild animals, even though doing so is against the law

semiaquatic – living partly on land and partly in water

weaned – made the young of a mammal accept food other than nursing milk

SELECTED BIBLIOGRAPHY

African Wildlife Foundation. "Hippopotamus." http://www.awf.org/content/wildlife/detail/hippopotamus.

Eltringham, S. K. *The Hippos: Natural History and Conservation.* London: Academic Press, 1999.

Huxley, Craig, and Jean-Christophe Jeauffre. *The Secret Life of Hippos.* DVD. Burbank, Calif.: Slingshot Entertainment, 2007.

San Diego Zoo. "Animal Bytes: Hippopotamus." http://www.sandiegozoo.org/animalbytes/t-hippopotamus.html.

Shefferly, Nancy. "*Hippopotamus amphibius.*" Animal Diversity Web. http://animaldiversity.ummz.umich.edu/accounts/Hippopotamus_amphibius/.

Stuart, Chris, and Tilde Stuart. *Field Guide to the Larger Mammals of Africa.* Cape Town: Struik Nature, 2007.

Nile cabbage is a fast-growing water plant that smothers algae, which helps keep hippo habitats clean.

INDEX